Copyright ® 2019 by Rythea Lee

Published by Zany Angels Press
Contact: www.rythea.com

All rights reserved.
No part of this book may be reproduced or transmitted in any form or by any means, or stored in a database or retrieval system, without permission in writing from the publisher.

Cover design and layout by Catherine White
Back cover photo by Kaitlin June

Thank you to all the people who made this online show and curriculum possible: Tom Knight, Jessica Prodis, Selena Goldberg, Will MacAdams, Colin Horowitz, Torielle Lee, Patrick Crowley, Rose Oceania, Samantha Burnell, Melissa Redwin, Chasa Foxvog, Liana Foxvog, Ishmael Dengate, Donna Jenson, Aishah Simmons, Cat White, Kent Alexander, Flávia Santos de Araújo, Carrie Ferguson, Tanya Rubins, Natasha Torres, Tammysha Ocasio, Christina Frei, Dana Wilde, Xinef Afraim, Diana Yourke, Anna Maynard, Yemar Pina, Leila Zainab, Juliet and Elizabeth Murphy, Lauren Hind, Lily Tucker, Rebecca Burwell, Michelle Huber, Rain Karen, Kaitlin June, Kendra Rosenblatt, Naomi Sparrow, Sanford Lewis, Cailin Reiken, Marcie Goldman, Kaia Jackson, Nikki Oquendo, Kalisto Gonzales, Shayna Chandelle Hesselgrave, and thank you so much to all my donors who donated on GoFundMe, I could not have made this without you!

Advice from a Loving Bitch Curriculum

Dedication:

May this process help people see self-hatred for what it is:

protection.

May this process help people see self-love for what it is:

the truth.

Advice from a Loving Bitch Curriculum

Experiential Learning for Groups and Individuals

INTRODUCTION

This curriculum is a comprehensive, in-depth program for individuals and groups to experience and learn about undoing patterns of self-hatred. It works directly with 20 episodes of a video series on YouTube called *Advice from a Loving Bitch*. As the title implies, it is a humorous, upbeat, edgy series that also tackles the very serious pain of internalized hatred.

This curriculum is an emotional education program appropriate for a wide range of ages (recommended 14 and up), life experiences, racial and class backgrounds, and learning styles. It can be applied to classroom learning, affinity groups, on-line programs, friend circles, mental health programs, health programs, and other group forums related to personal growth and community building. It is also a powerful tool for individuals who seek to use this curriculum as a workbook, to do the homework and answer the questions that go with each episode.

This curriculum is the step-by-step foundation for experiential learning that happens through:

- Theatrical experimentation
- Creative writing
- Visualization
- Therapeutic theory and demonstrations
- Creativity, Performance Art, and Storytelling
- Connecting with others on a similar path of personal growth

Rythea Lee, the creator of this curriculum and video series, uses her own process of healing, along with many guests, to illustrate how to dismantle internalized self-hatred. The videos show the healing process in real time while also explaining the technical details of how self-hatred functions for many people. The guests on the show demonstrate a range of how self-hatred sounds and looks, while also revealing a universal aspect of internalized pain. The video series introduces a long arc of how healing can unfold with the help of user-friendly tools and frameworks of understanding.

Rythea Lee has based aspects of this program and videos on her 25-year private practice with clients using a method called

Inner Bonding®, created by Dr. Margaret Paul and Dr. Erica Chopich. This modality is a spiritual and emotional framework for recovering from childhood wounds. It has been a powerful and effective method for helping people heal from early attachment wounds, depression, anxiety, addictions, fear of intimacy, and sexual, emotional, and physical abuse. Rythea has dedicated her life to assisting others to work consciously and lovingly with their protective survival patterns, to unearth the underlying joy and freedom that is each person's birthright.

Rythea's therapeutic perspective is combined with her life-long work and play as a performance artist in the videos of *Advice from a Loving Bitch.* She aims to make the concepts and language accessible and available to people who are drawn to therapeutic practices, but more importantly to those who have rarely or never been exposed to therapy and/or therapeutic ideas. She casts a large net out to a wide range of participants by making the curriculum and the videos funny, wacky, emotionally transparent, personal, and easy to follow.

The themes of the videos and curriculum are:
1. Episode 1: Externalizing the Self-Hating Voice
2. Episode 2: Stop Hating Your Inner Child
3. Episode 3: Self-Hatred is Universal

4. Episode 4: Getting Space from Self-Hatred
5. Episode 5: This is Self-Love
6. Episode 6: Inner Child Interviews
7. Episode 7: Your Essence is Lovable
8. Episode 8: Teens Weigh in on Love and Hate
9. Episode 9: Rock Star Rocks Self-Love
10. Episode 10: The Feelings Episode
11. Episode 11: Love is Universal
12. Episode 12: Love Demonstrated
13. Episode 13: Rythea's Story
14. Episode 14: Q and A Episode
15. Episode 15: A-holes are Everywhere
16. Episode 16: Creativity Explained
17. Episode 17: Racial Justice Episode
18. Episode 18: Asking for Help/Prayer song
19. Episode 19: Three Women Rising
20. Episode 20: Season Finale

A few important notes on this curriculum

This curriculum is not a replacement for therapy or in-depth support for trauma. It is an introduction to concepts that work well in conjunction with other support systems such as group process, one to one therapy, and peer support. It offers tools that open doors and once the doors begin to open, each participant must discover what other supports assist them to feel secure, safe, and understood. This may be something that participants learn about as they go. They might find they need more support to dig deeper into the concepts and that's a great thing to discover and research as needed.

Trigger warnings

Swearing

There is plenty of profanity in the *Advice from a Loving Bitch* videos (maybe the title hinted at this?) so that is good to know in advance. Rythea's irreverent style seems to include swearing but many other people on the show do this as well. Many folks who write in about appreciating the show seem to really appreciate the swearing but for those who teach this in more formal settings, it's good to know what you are working with. This course has been taught in high school and college settings without issue.

Abuse

Rythea talks openly about being a childhood sexual abuse survivor in Episodes 13 and 19. This is a big part of her story and she models many aspects of the healing process including overcoming the shame of the abuse. Particularly Episode 19 is about childhood sexual abuse directly and is talked about with two other guests who tell their story. Though there are no graphic details in that episode, it is something to be prepared for in terms of trigger warnings for participants if you are facilitating this curriculum.

Ideas in dealing with this are:

1. Warn people beforehand (the meeting before), that Episode 19 is on this subject so they can prepare themselves.

2. Leave ample time to discuss the ways people may be triggered after that episode.

3. Have a list of local resources for people who discover they want to look into this issue further.

4. If you are facilitating this curriculum and this is a difficult or triggering subject for you, bring in someone to support you as well as the class who is experienced around this subject.

If you are a CSA survivor and are concerned about being triggered by these episodes, read the description of the videos in this curriculum before you watch them and ascertain what kind of support you might need to watch them. You can also skip episodes and come back to them or skip them altogether.

Self-Harm

Though this series is upbeat, playful, and user-friendly, it can also provoke deep feelings and information. People who participate in this curriculum might find they tap into pain they did not know they had OR that they thought they had gotten over. If you are facilitating this curriculum with survivors of trauma, I suggest you do a screening beforehand to make sure participants are not in danger of self-harming during this process. If you have purchased this curriculum and are in danger of self-harm, please use this workbook with the aid and support of a therapist and/or mental health practitioner that you trust. Make sure they track your process as you go.

Choice

This curriculum is meant to empower people to take charge of their healing process and gain some mastery over their patterns. It's ESSENTIAL that you feel you have total choice over how you use this curriculum. You can read ahead and pick the episodes that seem important to your process. It does work best if you start from Episode 1 and build from there BUT you can skip around if that feels best for you. This curriculum is for you and for your healing. Be gentle and caring as you embark on this journey. Self-hatred is a protective pattern that has protected you; so, attempting to take those defenses down requires patience and love. Some of the episodes might be so powerful for you that you sit with that skill for several weeks before you go on to the next one. It's your choice! You can use this in whatever way supports you the most. It's here to help you.

Working in Connection

Ideally, you would use this curriculum with another person or group of people. The thing about self-hatred that we will discuss in this workbook is the fact that it thrives through staying hidden. This work is about bringing our hidden hatred out of hiding so we can look at it, track it back to our old wounds, and begin to see it for what it is- protection. Sometimes, we truly don't know how to love ourselves or show up for ourselves and that is why it would be great for this curriculum to be used in connection with other people. We need the input of others to help us see how good and precious we are as we work through this process. Also, when we see other people outing their self-hating voices, it is a profound shame-breaker! So, do it with a friend, a small group, your book group, your therapist, your 12 step friends- whoever is up for the challenge, if you can. If you end up doing this alone, is there one person you can share some of your learnings with now and then? That would be the most supportive way to do this. If not, then please use Rythea and the other people on the show as your support. Let them be examples of connection for you, because we ALL suffer from self-hatred.

THE CURRICULUM

Episode 1 of Advice from a Loving Bitch
Externalizing the Self-Hating Voice

The Essence of Episode 1: The core teaching of this episode is that everyone has a Self-Hating Voice. This Self-Hating Voice is an aspect of ourselves that judges, attacks, and tells us lies about who we are. This part of us is generally hidden and yet it causes deep pain and wounding. It tells us that we are ugly, unlovable, damaged, alone, crazy, weird, unworthy, unlikable, disgusting, different than others, and even evil or bad. The Self-Hating Voice is tricky, sneaky, and stays in charge by keeping us unconscious of its existence.

The Teaching: The Self-Hating Voice can only be healed by coming out and being seen. As long as we hurt ourselves in hiding, we cannot get any traction on changing these patterns of thought. In this episode, Rythea Lee, our host, acts out the messages of her Self-Hating Voice and through humor and irreverence, shows us how it looks to bring these voices into the light and out of hiding.

ASSIGNMENTS for Episode 1

The Assignment: The assignment in this episode is to externalize the Self-Hating Voice. Try one of these options.

1. Externalize through writing. Set a timer for 10 minutes and write out what your Self-Hating Voice sounds like in your head. Don't censor yourself, really go for the ugliness. This is like getting the venom out of a wound. Allow the Self-Hating Voice to criticize anything that comes to mind that you often tell yourself about such as your finances, sexuality, relationships, body, organizational skills, self-care, or your essential goodness. Let any subject be attacked even if it makes you cringe. You can do it. As hard as it is to see it and hear it, it's happening on the inside anyway. This is simply a way of breaking the denial around it.

2. Externalize by speaking it out loud. Try to say out loud what your Self-Hating Voice says to you in a similar fashion to how Rythea did it. You can video yourself doing it or just talk out loud for your own ears to hear. If you need privacy, do it in your car or in the middle of the woods or somewhere you know you have privacy. Really embody the way the Self-Hating Voice sounds in your head. Be wacky and silly

and exaggerate this part of you so you can really get a sense of it.

DISCUSSION for Episode 1

Reflections and questions to ponder alone, with a trusted friend, mentor, or group.

1. How does hearing the Self-Hating Voice make you feel in your body? Tense? Shaky? Spaced-out? Achy?

2. What emotions come up for you as you do this exercise? Mad, sad, scared, and ashamed?

3. Does externalizing this voice bring a feeling of relief such as laughing or the ability to breathe a little easier?

4. Can you see that some of things the voice is saying are lies?

5. Can you see a level of absurdity to it?

6. Does that voice remind you of anyone you know like a parent, a sibling, a teacher, or a friend?

7. Could you imagine saying these things to someone else?

Behind the Scenes of Episode 1

The voice in our head that rips us to pieces, what I call The Self-Hating Voice, loves to operate behind the scenes. It is the part of us that causes a huge portion of our internal pain and yet, it can only have control through our denial of its existence. It tells us we are bad, broken, unlovable, disgusting, not good enough, hopeless, etc. It gives us physical, emotional, and spiritual aches and pains but often, we can't find the source. We think it's coming from outside of us. We have internalized the judgments throughout our whole lives and now it's our hard drive. It runs when we are asleep. It runs when we are working. It runs when we are trying to love other people. It runs when we fail, when we lose, when we get lost.

That hatred WAS from outside of us when we were kids. We were taught all kinds of beliefs about ourselves that were damaging and critical such as, "you are not good enough," "you're ugly," "you're not thin enough," "you're not smart," "you're a burden," "you don't fit in," "you are lesser than others," "you don't deserve love and attention," "you can't succeed," "there's something wrong with you," and on and on but now we participate without noticing. We have internalized these beliefs to the point where we AGREE that we are bad and then life validates these beliefs. Many people have no idea that the pain is now an inside job, like a recording in our brain that is playing constantly.

Episode 1 of *Advice from a Loving Bitch* was my attempt at outing my Self-Hating Voice. I was terrified to do it, but I made myself do it (in the name of art). I put the camera on myself, put on hats, scarves, make-up, weird hairdos, and I said my shit out loud. I talked about how life sucks, I suck. How people hate me because I'm Jewish. How I'm essentially a bad person. How my art is meaningless. How even love is just a fantasy and I should give that up. Oh, and how I'm a money-losing loser. There's always that.
Let me tell you, once I got started, this thrill took over. I was SO RELIEVED to be saying it out loud. I started laughing my ass off. I had a good old time. And I was shocked by the things that were coming out of my mouth. I regularly do major self-care and self-help in my life, but I had no idea that my self-hatred sounded like that. I was amazed.

I invited my viewers to watch me do this and then try it on. It was the beginning of 20 episodes of my on-line show, and I was fully in it. I could feel that I was onto something very important. I was on a new edge and it was fresh. Alive and fresh with exposure and truth. Something to bite into, something transformational.

Next Step: Episode 2 will take you into the next step of the process of bringing your hidden self-hatred into the light for healing, so if you feel hungry to evolve onward, go to Episode 2.

Episode 2 of Advice from a Loving Bitch
Stop Hating Your Inner Child

The Essence of Episode 2: This episode illustrates whom the Self-Hating Voice is attacking within us. We learn that it goes after the most vulnerable, sweet, loving, open, innocent part of ourselves; the Inner Child. The Self-Hating Voice does this to protect us. It does this to keep our vulnerability from getting hurt. It uses terrible, scary tactics to make our Inner Child stay hidden.

The Teaching: Becoming aware of the Inner Child and how the Self-Hating Voice makes that child feel is an essential step in dismantling the self-hatred patterns within. We learned about the Self-Hating Voice and what is says, how it sounds, but who is it hurting inside? This is a central question and awareness.

Rythea demonstrates the Self-Hating Voice criticizing the Inner Child (her daughter plays the Inner Child in episode 2). She also shows the Inner Child, its innocence and susceptibility to getting hurt. When we begin to understand who our Self-Hating Voice is hurting, we can plant a seed of compassion in the whole pattern. We can begin to tap into the reality of what self- hatred is really doing to us on the inside. We can wake up to a deeper understanding of why and how we use self-hatred to feel safe.

ASSIGNMENTS for Episode 2

The Assignment: The assignment in this episode is to connect your Self-Hating Voice to your Inner Child. Try one of these options.

1. Find a photo of yourself when you were a cute little kid. One where you think you look super adorable. If you have trouble seeing your cuteness, pick one where you look innocent or vulnerable. Yell out loud at the picture of yourself with your Self-Hating Voice. Say all the things you say to yourself in your daily life about being unlovable, unattractive, incompetent, unworthy, and not good enough. Mean things about money, time, energy, health, whatever it is you think in your mind that causes you pain and stress. Make the connection between your Self-Hating Voice and your Inner Child (keep your eyes on the photo). Feel into what it must be like for that part of you to be talked to this way. Notice how the messages make that precious Inner Child FEEL. The feelings are the most important part. Mean words = feelings of shame, grief, terror, and anger. Can you see the connection?

2. If you find it very difficult to do this exercise out loud then do it through writing. Look at the photo of little you and write down the insults. Let them rip. Let them flow. Don't hold back and then take a few minutes to notice how that makes your Inner Child feel. Look at the photo and imagine that the feelings you are having are his/her/their feelings. That little child inside of you. That's who is getting attacked. Do your best to make that connection.

DISCUSSION for Episode 2
Reflections and questions to ponder alone, with a trusted friend, mentor, or group.

1. How did it feel to see Rythea yell at the child in this episode?

2. Can you tap into your Inner Child and how she, he, or they feel when you run your Self-Hating Voice?

3. Can you feel the relationship between the Self-Hating Voice and your Inner Child?

4. What does your Inner Child look like? How old is he, she, or they?

5. Could you imagine turning your Self-Hating Voice on a real child? What do you imagine that child would feel if you did?

Behind the Scenes of Episode 2

The "Inner Child" is a popular term these days and seems to mean many things to many people. In my work, it's the unwounded, untouched child inside you who is completely intact even after living through the pain and hurt of growing up. That means that the innocent, bright, loving, open, tender, and creative baby we were born as is still inside of us. There is a soul spark of goodness that is ever-present even if it is deeply buried.

Our Inner Child still wants connection, love, expression, and kindness. He, she, or they are waiting for us and knows when we are on track with loving ourselves or off track and being mean to ourselves.

In Episode 2, I was very excited to illustrate in 3-D how our Self-Hating Voice goes after our Inner Child and causes us deep heartbreak. I had my daughter play my Inner Child because she is so clearly vital and full of love. Then I showed how my Self-Hating Voice sounds in my head, cursing, criticizing, and trying to hide that child. It didn't happen in real life, it was all editing, don't worry.

On film, you got to see the back and forth of the dialogue of The Self-Hating Voice and The Inner Child and it turned out to be truly disturbing and oddly funny. I think the humor comes from the absurdity of the dynamic and the horror of seeing it so front and center. There's this kind of "What???" that happens when you bring this dynamic out of hiding. When I showed the videos on a big screen, this episode got a big laugh because of the recognition of how tragic it is to yell at a sweet, darling, playful child.

Next Step: Once you have some grasp of the dynamic between your Self-Hating Voice and your Inner Child, Episode 3 brings in specials guests to show you that you are not alone.

Episode 3 of Advice from a Loving Bitch
Self-Hatred is Universal

The Essence of Episode 3: This episode features guests from different walks of life acting out their Self-Hating Voices on screen. There are 5 guests and each one has their own special way of hating on themselves. You get to see the humor and absurdity of how we berate ourselves. You get to see how sad it is, how tragic, how funny, and how charged with life force it can be. You can also see how beautiful, alive, and unique each person is even while they are revealing their worst inner critic.

The Teaching: The beauty and power of this practice is getting the details of the Self-Hating Voice out in the open to dismantle:

- The lies we tell ourselves as if they are true
- The unconscious beliefs from childhood we continue to put on ourselves into adulthood
- The messages of cultural oppressions that get internalized regarding sexism, racism, ageism, ableism, and homophobia

- The stuck perceptions held in place by shame and hiding
- The painful mechanisms of thinking we use to protect ourselves from getting hurt

ASSIGNMENT for Episode 3

The Assignment: The assignment in this episode is to share your Self-Hating Voice with someone you trust.

1. Find a friend you trust and speak your Self-Hating Voices out loud to each other. Offer compassionate responses to each other such as "Wow, your Self-Hating Voice is a real meany!" Or "That is so untrue!" Have a good laugh at the lies your Self-Hating Voice is saying. Sometimes you may share this while feeling lots of shame and that's normal since you've been hiding this for a long time. Sometimes it helps to exaggerate the voice just to amp up the absurdity of it. Allow the shame to be there, allow it to move through you. It's the hiding that keeps it stuck and frozen.

2. If you can't find someone to do this with, video yourself doing the Self-Hating Voice and watch it. See the comic value if possible or at least aim for compassion. It helps to think "Oh, this is what I tell myself in order to feel safe."

DISCUSSION for Episode 3
Reflections and questions to ponder alone, with a trusted friend, mentor, or group.

1. Which person in Episode 3 did you relate to the most and why?

2. Could you see how absurd some of the Self-Hating Voices were when others were doing it?

3. What emotions did you notice while watching other people expose their self-hatred?

4. Did you have compassion for the people who were hating themselves?

5. Could you see the humor in the whole process?

6. What seems to be the scariest thing about letting the Self-Hating Voice come out into the open?

Behind the Scenes of Episode 3

Episode 3 was one of the most thrilling episodes of Advice from a Loving Bitch for me because it was the first-time special guests came on to contribute to my vision. I was no longer doing it alone. It wasn't just about me. It was the beginning of broadening the scope of the show.

My five guests, Kent, Flávia, Carrie, Rose, and Tom, boldly show us what their self-hate looks like. They do it with verve, honesty, humor, and with real pain. I was so surprised at how gung-ho my guests were on film once I gave them the assignment. They proved my essential premise which is: *acting out our mean voices is cathartic and helpful.*

When we play the hatred out loud fully, without holding back, we can finally see the shape, the sound, and the specifics our self-hatred uses and get a glaring good look at it. Usually when self-hatred is in our heads, we don't know what it's really saying because it goes by so quick and is so jumbled up with our feelings that it has a quiet agonizing hold on us. It's mostly not conscious. But even when it is conscious, we still have such secrecy and shame around it that we can't look at it clearly. This seeing and hearing of the Self-Hating Voice is paramount. It's the wild and wacky beginning of perspective. An inch of space from the pain and lies.

My guests came on the show and kicked it out. Each person's Self-Hating Voice was totally unique and yet very universal. All of them, without fail, were funny to hear. I think that is because we all relate so much.

The Self-Hating Voice seems absurd and desperate once you see it in full color. It becomes clear that this voice was born from coping and pain. We begin to feel a little sorry for this voice, we see its fear, its need to feel powerful, its need to control, and maybe even its need to be loved.

Next Step: Once you see how universal self-hatred is and get a sense that you are not alone in this affliction, you can move on to the concept of distancing and healing the Self-Hating Voice in Episode 4.

Episode 4 of Advice from a Loving Bitch
Getting Space from Self-Hatred

The Essence of Episode 4: Episode 4 is a review of the first 3 episodes in terms of covering the Self-Hating Voice, the Inner Child, and then witnessing other people's self-hatred as a universal issue, pain, problem, and/or pattern. Episode 4 also highlights a talk with artist and activist Kent Alexander, discussing the feelings and the experience of starting to deal directly with the Self-Hating Voice and asking the question, can we heal these patterns? Can we get distance from the self-hatred?

The Teaching: Self-hatred is a strategy we have learned to protect ourselves from unbearable feelings. Can we witness the mechanism of that kind of protection within ourselves? Kent and Rythea share about having the experience of getting more and more distance from the voice in their heads that wants to destroy them and/or sabotage them. Seeing self-hatred for what it is happens when we recognize the feelings and the pain underneath the self-hatred. This episode entertains the idea that the things the Self-Hating Voice are saying are not true and in fact, the Self-Hating Voice needs to be seen as the terrified and deluded part of you it truly is.

ASSIGNMENTS for Episode 4

The Assignment: The assignment in this episode is designed to help you see the correlation between what your Self-Hating voice says inside your head and what you feel emotionally throughout the day or in your life in general. All three parts of this assignment go together.

1. Make a chart and on one side of the chart, write out the mean things you say to yourself. It could be things such as nobody likes you, you are not worthy of a romantic partner, you are a total failure, you are ugly and unattractive, you suck in every way, and so on.

2. On the other side of the chart write down how each of those things you say to yourself makes you feel. Write the feelings such as mad, sad, scared, ashamed, hopeless, lonely, helpless, etc. Notice the obvious correlation between what the Self-Hating Voice says and what you feel emotionally. Take the time to tune into this connection as you make this chart. Don't do the exercise just from your mind, let the words echo into your physical body and emotions as well.

3. Do an 8-minute free write starting with the prompt "If I let the lies go then...." and see what comes out when you start with this sentence. Don't worry about it sounding good or making sense or being grammatically correct. Just write from the heart and when you get stuck, write the sentence again, "If I let the lies go then...." and see what follows. Don't stop writing until the 8 minutes are up.

4. If you are doing this work with a friend, read the writing out loud to each other and listen without giving advice. If you are doing this alone, then read it to yourself out loud and notice how it feels to entertain the idea of letting this pattern of self-hatred go.

DISCUSSION for Episode 4
Reflections and questions to ponder alone, with a trusted friend, mentor, or group.

1. Review the skills we have learned so far from the videos. Go over the understanding of externalizing the Self-Hating Voice and the relationship between the Self-Hating Voice and the Inner Child.

2. Discuss and review the idea that everyone has a Self-Hating voice and how that voice keeps its power by being hidden.

3. What do you think would happen if you stopped believing the Self-Hating Voice?

4. Are you scared of something happening if you stopped hating on yourself?

5. Could you imagine having a little bit of space or distance from your self-hatred?

6. What are some of the feelings that you are aware of when you name the messages of the Self-Hating Voice? Do you

feel mad, sad, scared, or ashamed? What other feelings come to mind?

7. What is the connection you see between the Self-Hating Voice and your emotions throughout your day or in your life?

8. Is there a feeling you are avoiding by hating on yourself, such as loneliness, terror, helplessness, or grief?

Behind the Scenes of Episode 4

Episode 4 was exciting for a few reasons. First, I shot the episode in my bathroom and went into a super charged creative state while filming. I reviewed the skills we had learned in Episodes 1-3 (using little wooden dolls) to make sure we were all up to speed. I was blown away at this point to discover that people on the internet were engaging in my show, doing the assignments, and writing me emails about huge insights based on the teachings so far. A few fans even hated themselves on film and sent it to me. So, I was pumped up and ready to carry on.

Also exciting was the visit from Kent Alexander to discuss the issue of perspective with me. The question we looked at was how do we get enough distance from our self-hatred to realize that the messages it runs are hurtful lies? We discussed the idea that we could see the self-hatred, hear the self-hatred, and still know it was not the truth. We both had glimpsed in large ways that our self-hatred was delusional and terrified. We had begun to offer love and compassion to this part of ourselves.

A potent moment for me on this episode was when Kent admits that he was beaten as a child and explains that, although he could block out that physical assault, he could never block out the self-hatred that followed the abuse year after year. He pinpoints the insidious and pervasive nature of self-hatred and how it often seems impossible to get rid of.

At the end of the episode, Kent and I had a dance party, as I do at the end of every episode. Something about dancing with Kent was very touching to me because our joy together felt so clearly hard-won. We were not just surviving by ignoring what we had lived through; we were finding joy by facing our pain. That seemed to be the core of our message. Looking at the self-hatred was the doorway through it. The pathway into the pain was leading us out of the pain and into freedom.

Next Step: Hopefully by this episode you can imagine in some small way that you could get some breathing space from your Self-Hating Voice. The next step is to actually love that part of you! This is illustrated in Episode 5.

Episode 5 of Advice from a Loving Bitch
This is Self-Love

The Essence of Episode 5: This Episode is a turning point in the series, where a loving voice and presence is invited into the process of healing. You are introduced to the Loving Adult and shown how it cares for and brings compassion to the Self-Hating Voice.

The Teaching: At this point of the series, we have dug our teeth into self-hatred and shined a big light on its voice. We have talked it out loud, written it, seen others do it, and learned about its powerful hold on our psyche. Now the Loving Adult is introduced, the part of us that can speak back to the Self-Hating Voice.

Rythea demonstrates how this might look by playing both parts and having them talk to each other. The Loving Adult tells the Self-Hating Voice that she is going to be retired, that she will no longer be in control of Rythea's life. The Loving Adult explains that Rythea is no longer in danger and does not need that level of vigilance and self-criticism in order to survive. The Self-Hating Voice puts up a solid fight, explaining how it won't step down and how unsafe it is to consider the idea.

Rythea shows us some of the underlying emotional material that is attached to this dialogue. She shows how charged the conversation might be. The Loving Adult brings understanding, kindness, and caring to the Self-Hating Voice while validating what a good job the Self-Hating Voice has done in the name of protection and survival.

ASSIGNMENTS for Episode 5

The Assignment: The assignment in this episode invites you to try the dialogue between these two parts of yourself, the Self-Hating Voice and your Loving Adult.

1. Speak the Self-Hating Voice out loud or through writing. Allow it to criticize, worry, attack, and say scary things about anything it wants, especially the things that have been bothering you lately.

2. Invoke your Loving Adult. If this is hard to do, you can imagine a loving presence of someone or something coming through you, whom you experience as 100% unconditionally loving. For example, your childhood dog, a deity like Jesus or The Goddess, Glinda the Good Witch, or a nature being like a loving tree or mountain.

3. Speak back to the Self-Hating Voice. Let it know that you are taking over and its job is done. Go back and forth until you feel some level of resolution or understanding about the fight inside yourself. You don't have to fix it or solve it but do open to learning about this internal conflict.

4. If you absolutely cannot invoke a Loving Adult presence, find someone in your life who could act that out for you. Have them speak to your Self-Hating Voice. Write down what you learned from this experiment!

5. Try it again. Once someone else has done if for you, try it for yourself. Don't give up.

DISCUSSION for Episode 5
Reflections and questions to ponder alone, with a trusted friend, mentor, or group.

1. What was it like for you to see Rythea roll around in a dance studio and speak more from her body than her mind?

2. What did you relate to when you saw her role-playing between the Loving Adult and the Self-Hating Voice?

3. Did you think she could really retire that part?

4. Could you imagine being that loving to your Self-Hating Voice?

5. What feelings came up for you watching her play both parts?

6. Did you think there was some level of resolution or healing between the two parts Rythea played?

7. What would you do differently if you did that dialogue?

8. Is there someone you would fashion your Loving Adult after?

Behind the Scenes of Episode 5

Episode 5 felt life changing for me. I had never acted out my Self-Hating Voice and my Loving Adult parts with such clarity, even though I had been journaling about them and doing therapy on them for years. Something about acting it out in 3-D characters brought fresh understanding.

I saw I had the strength to retire the Self-Hating Voice. I had enough empathy inside of me to understand that voice and give it respect and reverence. I finally grasped that unbearable pain the Self-Hating Voice was shielding me from, how hard it had worked all my life to keep me alive. I saw its terror, its trauma, its horror. I wanted to help it to finally relax.

My Self-Hating Voice put up a good fight on screen. It did not want to step down. It wasn't willing to give up the reigns and was not convinced that my Loving Adult was strong enough for the job.

Tears were shed. I felt terror and rage during filming. I saw the internal fight for what it was, a strategy that had saved my life. I felt such sadness for how hard I had been working to be ok all my life. It was a pivot point.

The thing about this series for me was that I was living the series as I made it. I had done all the groundwork in terms of feeling and healing my deepest issues for 20 years, but now I was modeling it with total commitment. I was letting my audience into a private process. The risky business of being seen in that way, allowing my vulnerability to be witnessed, was supremely powerful. I learned as I filmed. I changed as I embodied what I was teaching. Most importantly, I proved to myself that the process could work, was working, and had done its work on me.

Next Step: You have come so far. You have heard and seen your Self-Hating Voice. You have spoken back to that part with your Loving Adult or had someone else do it on your behalf. Now you can go on to Episode 6 where you can explore some important aspects of your Inner Child.

Episode 6 of Advice from a Loving Bitch
Inner Child Interviews

The Essence of Episode 6: This episode takes a very unofficial poll about the Inner Child from people on the streets of Northampton, MA, the town where Rythea lives.

The Teaching: Rythea and her special guest, Tanya Rubins, hit the streets with a camera and microphone and asked random people:

"Do you have an Inner Child?"
"What's your definition of the Inner Child?"
"What is something weird about your Inner Child?"
"How old is your Inner Child?"
"Who shuts your Inner Child down?"

What Rythea and Tanya learned is that many people do feel that they have an Inner Child. People described that part of them in a wide range of ways but often enthusiastically and joyfully. There seemed a common theme of the Inner Child being innocent, carefree, vital, bold, and courageous. Not one person they interviewed said they did not have an Inner Child.

After talking to total strangers in Northampton, Rythea and Tanya felt hopeful about how open people were to their questions and were excited by the heart-centered responses they received.

This episode raises questions for the viewers as well, offering the chance to consider their Inner Child, if they have one, and if they resonate and relate to the answers people gave.

ASSIGNMENTS for Episode 6

The Assignment: This assignment is designed to help you tune in to your Inner Child. All parts of this assignment go together.

1. Take five minutes and connect with your Inner Child. This means picture yourself as a child at any age that comes to you and feel into this part of yourself.

2. Ask yourself, how old is my Inner Child?

3. Ask yourself, what does my Inner Child really like to do? You can write your answers down if that is helpful. You can also allow the child to answer these questions directly.

4. Find someone in your life and ask them the same questions. Have a dialogue with this person about your inner kids. Explore together what your Inner Children are like, how they feel inside, how they express themselves, and what is surprising to each of you about your IC. See what is similar between your Inner Children and what is different.

DISCUSSION for Episode 6
Reflections and questions to ponder alone, with a trusted friend, mentor, or group.

1. What was it like for you to watch other people talk about their Inner Child?

2. Did you relate to certain people on the episode and not others?

3. Do you find it difficult to imagine your Inner Child or is it easy for you?

4. Do you see other people's Inner Child when you look at them?

5. Can you share things about your Inner Child like what he, she, or they like, dislike, want, don't want, and/or are drawn to? What are their core qualities such as funny, mischievous, quiet, creative, bold, fearless, etc.?

6. Could you imagine asking other people in your life about their Inner Child? Do you think they would know what you are talking about?

Behind the Scenes of Episode 6

This episode was a total blast. I've never gone onto the streets of anywhere and tried to interview people. I was so nervous! I thought people would totally reject our advances with our fake microphone and real-life camera but in fact, people were totally up for it. The questions we asked about people's Inner Child were embraced, and folks thought good and hard about their answers. Every single person we asked said they did, in fact, have an Inner Child and that was a shock. I thought people were going to say, "I don't relate to that question," but no one did. Was it because Northampton was and is a mostly white privileged progressive town and the Inner Child is a privileged New Age concept? I couldn't help but wonder. I had to be honest that in entering my own town, I was not getting a good sample. Since filming this show, I have learned much more about racism and classism and I now wish I had gone to a diverse city or town. I have regrets and that is one of them. In my enthusiasm, I picked what was easy for me and that was to go to the town I lived in. As the show progressed through the months, I learned more about how to push my own edges, get uncomfortable, and reach outside my own race and class blinders.

The valuable part of this episode was witnessing people being vulnerable while being put on the spot. I saw the child in each person I interviewed and that was heartening. I saw that there is a joy that emanates from people that is innocent and eager. The street performer we interviewed shared an incredible song that captured the connection between the Inner Child and creativity. I also loved the last person I interviewed who ended up dancing on the street, acting out her Inner Child's movement, so refreshing and real. Tanya Rubins was such an all-in co-pilot for this episode. She made me laugh with her sincerity and went after people on the streets with total gusto. Sharing the load made it much more fun. I'd do it again in a heartbeat.

Next Step: I hope you feel some connection with your Inner Child now. The next episode continues this exploration inside ourselves by going to the Essence of who we are.

Episode 7 of Advice from a Loving Bitch
Your Essence is Lovable

The Essence of Episode 7: The reason we are exploring our Inner Child is because it points us to who we are, our essence. Our essence expresses our core qualities that emanate outward no matter what we are doing or saying. It's our unspoken nature or our spiritual presence.

The Teaching: This episode has a newborn baby in it! This is so you can see how precious a baby is before he, she, or they are talking, moving, or doing anything. In the episode, I explain that each of us are valuable JUST BECAUSE and for no other reason. We are lovable and worthy of care just because we exist. This is a radical teaching for most of us in a world where getting things done, being useful, successful, or busy is considered most important. We all have learned that we have to earn our lovability and most of us develop self-hatred based on this way of measuring. In this prove-yourself model of being worthy, we all fall short.

The teaching of this episode is that we all have an essence and it is the lovable, worthy, pure, innocent part of ourselves. We need to see it, feel it, acknowledge it, and eventually, love it.

This episode also has a skit about the Inner Child in it that is a satire about the Inner Child being an actual organ in our bodies that needs love and care. This part of the show is designed to make you laugh at how real the Inner Child can seem.

ASSIGNMENTS for Episode 7

The Assignment: This assignment invites you to connect with an even younger version of your Inner Child, your newborn baby. All parts of this assignment go together.

1. Take a moment and imagine yourself as a newborn baby.

2. Then imagine yourself as an adult picking up that baby and holding that baby close.

3. Take the time to bring love and honoring to that baby part of you. If it helps to hold a stuffed animal or doll, go for it.

4. If this assignment feels very difficult, then imagine your little newborn baby as a little puppy, a kitten, a bunny rabbit, or something you could love easily. Hold that being with kindness.

DISCUSSION for Episode 7

Reflections and questions to ponder alone, with a trusted friend, mentor, or group.

1. What was it like to see Rythea holding that newborn baby? Did you feel empathy, care, and love towards the baby or disgust, anger, and/or numbness?

2. What is your experience with newborn babies? Do you like them?

3. Can you imagine yourself as a newborn baby? Do you think you are cute and cuddly? Or do you have disdain or indifference?

4. What are some of your core essence qualities such as curious, tender, generous, wild, enthusiastic, playful, etc.? If you can't feel your essence qualities, do you know someone who could describe yours for you?

5. What do you see as the connection between your newborn essence and loving yourself? Or hating yourself? How do those things connect?

6. Can you see the essence qualities in other people?

7. Do you think you are inherently lovable?

8. Do you think you have to perform in a certain way to be lovable?

Behind the Scenes of Episode 7

The remarkable thing about the making of my show for me was that there was always a flow. I would get an idea for each episode and all the details would fall into place. In Episode 7, I knew I needed a newborn baby and my friends who had a new baby said, "Sure, you can use my baby for this." I was so happy they would allow this and even let me post it online. What a coo!

The baby was super mellow while I filmed. He made all these cute faces and sounds and looked right into the camera. I was delighted that he was modeling exactly what I was talking about, innate cuteness! I was explaining that we are ALL born this cute, this lovable, this worthy of care. I was pretty sure that the baby was proving everything I was saying to be true just by hanging out in my arms.

Then, for this episode, I posted a skit about the Inner Child I had filmed a year or so earlier with my collaborator Rose Oceania. It was a news program on the whereabouts of the Inner Child. I describe the Inner Child (IC) as located in our bodies, the same as our vital organs. I talk about how, just like our organs, we need to attend to our IC in order to stay in good health. While I give reports on the IC, Rose crawls all over me just like an Inner Child. I always love to bring my performance art into the episodes if possible. So, it's performance art within performance art. My favorite.

The message that loving ourselves for no other reason than because we exist is essential in the self-loving piece of our learning. We need to be able to be enough just as we are, in order to love ourselves. We need to be able to take care of ourselves without conditions, judgments, and demands. Our essence will always be shining through, no matter the ups and downs of our worldly achievements. Being in touch with our essential nature will help us find a way into self-love, a way into seeing ourselves for who we truly are.

Next Step: This episode has helped you contact your essence, something that is always present in your life. Now you can check out some teenagers who are learning the same thing and remember the impact of the teen years on how we love ourselves.

Episode 8 of Advice from a Loving Bitch
Teens Weigh in on Love and Hate

The Essence of Episode 8: This episode demonstrates the power and transformational tool of facing the Self-Hating Voice and developing a Loving Adult while in a facilitated group setting. It gives real-life examples of high school students who have used *Advice from a Loving Bitch* to connect with each other, grow, and heal as a community.

The Teaching: This episode takes an unexpected turn when Rythea visits a group of her fans and films an episode with them. They are students at the Paulo Fueire Social Justice High School in Holyoke, Massachusetts who have been watching her episodes as part of a class called "Being Human." The teens are crazy about the show and so Rythea suggested to the teachers that she come do an episode in their classroom.

Rythea discovers, much to her surprise, that the students have had some major emotional shifts due to watching her show. She interviews several of them and learns about what is possible when teenagers face their mean inner critic as a group, with the help of their loving teachers.

ASSIGNMENTS for Episode 8

The Assignment: This assignment helps you connect to your teenage years of self-hatred and the Loving Adult that can step in. All parts of this assignment go together.

1. After watching Episode 8, write down what touched you or moved you from listening to the teenagers. Write without stopping for 10 minutes

2. Write down what you related to in terms of the Self-Hating Voices of the teens.

3. Write down the loving messages that you are starting to say to yourself from your Loving Adult. What does your Loving Adult sound like these days?

4. If you are an adult, reflect on how you might have benefitted from a class on self-hatred and self-love when you were a teen.

5. If you are a teenager, reflect on how a class like this in your school might benefit you now.

DISCUSSION for Episode 8
Reflections and questions to ponder alone, with a trusted friend, mentor, or group.

1. What do you remember about being a teenager and dealing with self-hatred? (If you are a teenager, talk about your experience now).

2. What do you remember about loving yourself when you were a teenager?

3. What did your parents or other trusted adults teach you about loving yourself or hating yourself?

4. What do you think is important about the teenage years in terms of learning about this process (i.e. The Inner Child, the Self-Hating Voice, The Loving Adult, our essence)?

5. What is particularly powerful about teenage years regarding growing self-esteem and interacting with others?

6. What was or is your transition experience of becoming an adult? How did self-hatred factor into that?

Behind the Scenes of Episode 8

Episode 8 blew my mind. I was not expecting the teenagers at the Paulo Freire Social Justice High School to tell me the things they told me. I thought they would be funny and interesting (and they were) but they were deep and honest at a level that surprised me in the best way. One teen talked about how she had always told herself that the bad things she had lived through were all her fault, but how watching the show made her stop blaming herself. After my interview with her, I just wept.

Several teens talked about how they could now talk back to their self-hatred and tell it to stop, to shut up, and that it was wrong. They saw another way to approach their critical beliefs besides buying into them.

Something important to note is that they watched my shows during a weekly class and the teachers facilitated discussions and assignments before and after each episode. As I made the show, it was being used as a modality for this class called "Being Human."

I was friends with one of the teachers, so each week, she would give me reports on how the show was affecting the students. They talked about how students got more and more comfortable expressing their feelings and thoughts as the weeks progressed (they watched one episode a week). The students also began to get closer to each other through the subject matter and a community was being built. They told me that most of the students had suffered heavy traumas as children and in their homes, and so the work of the show was giving them a way to process.

Even after I made this episode with them, they continued to follow along with my show. This amazed me and gave me the strength and incentive to keep going.

Teenagers really move me because they are so vulnerable and so strong. They are children, but they are individuals who need autonomy. They are expressive and protective. They are fierce and need allies. This experience reminded me of my inner teenager and how the roots of my self-hatred were solidifying at that time in my life. I wondered what a class like this would have done for me. These teens showed me, it would have had an impact.

Next Step: This was a visit to the teen years of our development. Let's take a humor break in the next episode by learning about false beliefs from a real-life rock star.

Episode 9 of Advice from a Loving Bitch
Rock Star Rocks Self-Love

The Essence of Episode 9: This episode brings in the concept of false beliefs; the things we tell ourselves that are not true and therefore hurt us. Rythea airs her first music video in this episode in a song called "Low Frequency Thought-Forms" to illustrate through humor how wrong our thoughts can be.

The Teaching: Like the Self-Hating Voice, false beliefs are often created from distress in childhood, from cultural and societal biases, and from getting physically, emotionally, and spiritually wounded in general as human beings. Painful things happen to us and we form beliefs from those experiences. For example, if we were teased as a child, we might decide that there is something wrong with us. If we had a parent who didn't pay attention to us, we might decide that we are unworthy of attention or love. If we lost a person in our lives, we might decide that people will always leave. Children especially, often make sense of pain by blaming themselves and forming beliefs around that blame.

People and society also actively teach us false beliefs such as being attractive looks this or that way, being smart means you make this much money, showing big feelings is weak, being a minority is not as good as being a majority, being quiet is boring, or all kinds of zillions of false beliefs that we think are normal or true.

This episode asks you to name some false beliefs that you hold as true and see how they feel to you, to write them down and look at them. Rythea performs the song "Low Frequency Thought-forms" to make you laugh at your absurd ideas, see them more clearly, in the hopes that you start questioning the validity of the beliefs. Are they true? If they hurt you this much, is it possible they are not true?

ASSIGNMENTS for Episode 9

The Assignment: This assignment is all about false beliefs and truths, helping you see and experience the difference. All parts of this assignment go together.

1. Write down 10 false beliefs on a piece of paper.

2. Next to each belief, write down the truth about that belief. For example: If you wrote a false belief like "I will never have what I want", then next to it, write down the truth, even if it feels fake, such as "I can have what I want" or "I already have many things that I want." Notice how it feels to write down the truth.

3. Do some writing about where each belief might have come from, some childhood experiences, and/or some key moments in your life that might have caused you to believe these things.

4. Write about what it would feel like if you gave up one of these false beliefs and committed to the truth. Could you? What would that be like?

DISCUSSION for Episode 9
Reflections and questions to ponder alone, with a trusted friend, mentor, or group.

1. What was it like hearing Rythea name the false beliefs in this episode? Did you resonate with any of them? Which ones?

2. What are some false beliefs you are aware of that you tell yourself all the time?

3. Where did you learn some of your false beliefs?

4. Can you imagine bringing in the truth about your false belief? What if you stopped believing you were bad, wrong, ugly, ruined, stuck, or alone? What do you imagine might happen?

5. Do you think you have any choice over your beliefs?

6. How do you think false beliefs might have served you in the past? Did they help you cope or protect yourself?

7. Do you think loving yourself or believing the truth about yourself is possible?

8. Do you think loving yourself and believing the truth about yourself is dangerous?

9. Ask someone else about a false belief you have about yourself and ask them what the truth might be. Often, we can't see how our low frequency thought-forms are hurting us.

Behind the Scenes of Episode 9

Making my first music video for Episode 9 was a teenage dream come true. When I was a teenager, I had this rock star character I did for my friends that would make them laugh. I had an air guitar back then and did jump splits. What an absolute hoot to recreate that character for this show. Using a trampoline helped. Wearing polka-dotted tights really helped. Teasing my hair was just the thing. I wrote the song "Low Frequency Thought-forms" years ago and in this episode about false beliefs, it suddenly seemed a perfect fit.

My rock star with a (very bad) English accent explains on this episode that false beliefs are things we believe about ourselves that are not true, and because they are not true, they "bloody well hurt." I introduce the concept that lies are painful (such a basic idea but lost on most of us). When we tell ourselves that we are wrong, left out, a failure, unworthy, unlovable, etc., it hurts because it goes against what we instinctively know to be true. We begin to understand this when we FEEL how the false beliefs affect us. The deep lies we have internalized are one of the main causes of the pain in our lives. This is what this episode aims to reveal.

The song I sing in my music video talks about the real beauty underneath the low frequency thought-forms. How I know deep down that I am a light in the world even though my mind tells me I suck and encourages me to eat ice cream to numb the pain.

One of my biggest take-aways in making this episode is something I learn over and over, that laughter is medicine. I laughed my way through this filming process while also really getting that the pain is real. It's very hard to reevaluate a false belief I took on amid deep pain. When my mother neglected me when I was little, I believed I was too much, too needy, and not likable. I really took it on. I believed that for so many years. Undoing the false belief that I was the problem required me to go back and feel the pain of how the belief got created. That took support, courage, and faith. I had to build a life of self-care that could hold that neglected child. I had to see that little girl who was so terrified and tell her the truth. She was not too much and she was not too needy. She was not unlikable. Correcting the false belief is not a heady venture. It's a feeling venture. All the way, deep down, into the heart of things.

Next Step: False beliefs are powerful and now you have named some of yours. The next step is to allow yourself FEELINGS. Are you ready? Go to Episode 10.

Episode 10 of Advice from a Loving Bitch
The Feelings Episode

The Essence of Episode 10: This episode is all about having feelings. Rythea's co-host, Samantha Burnell, is a counselor and teacher who co-teaches Rythea's Peer Counseling courses with her. They show in real time, real feelings and THEN show their kids having real feelings too!

The Teaching: Feelings are a huge part of being human, a core component of the healing process, and an essential piece of undoing self-hatred. Samantha and Rythea explain that they have been practicing Peer Counseling together for several years, a modality where they take turns listening to the other person and allowing feelings to be shared and expressed. They break down their approach to emotional health on the video:

1. *Feelings are Life Force:* When we are feeling our feelings (allowing our emotions to be expressed) we feel most alive. Happiness is an enlivening feeling but even when we are feeling painful feelings such as fear or anger, we become present. When we don't allow ourselves to feel, our life-force is then being used to stop our feelings, to hold them down, and that's when we get stuck and tied up inside. It

stops the flow of energy and authentic expression. It also makes it so there is not much life force left over for being alive and present.

2. *Feelings Will Not Kill You:* When we were kids, there were certain feelings that were acceptable to the adults in our lives and when we felt the other feelings, we got shamed, blamed, ridiculed, left alone, or ignored. We had to get rid of those feelings in order to survive, in order to receive love. Then we grow up, and we often can't find those feelings anymore. As we start to reclaim our feelings, we might feel like we are going to die (because that is how it felt as a kid) but we are not. It's just feelings!

3. *Feeling Your Feelings Takes Practice:* Just beginning to know what we are feeling and being able to name what we are feeling can be a big deal, something we need to learn to do and practice. We might notice that we open and close, feel and then don't feel, and that's normal. Eventually, we will get used to feeling alive more of the time than shut down. The shutdown experience can become so uncomfortable once we compare it to being open, that we become willing to use the tools we know in order to get back to the aliveness. Often, we start to crave the open state.

Feelings are a life-long condition; they are not going to go away. So, this practice of allowing them to be heard and expressed is about having a healthy relationship to our humanity.

Samantha and Rythea show the Peer Counseling process on film and show the discharge (release) of feeling fear, shame, anger, sadness, and happiness. Then their children come on to show you some feelings, sharing the idea that children would benefit most from being allowed to express all their feelings, the whole range.

The underlying idea of emotional health regarding self-hatred is, if we allow ourselves to feel the pain and pleasure that we naturally feel, it helps dismantle the stuck-ness and shut-down that self-hatred thrives on. Self-hatred is often connected to a bunch of feelings we never got to feel. As we move and share those feelings, we begin to understand some of the origins of our internalized hatred.

ASSIGNMENTS for Episode 10

The Assignment: This assignment is designed to help you contact your emotions and share them with someone who cares. All parts of this assignment go together.

1. Write down the five main feelings: mad, sad, scared, happy, and ashamed. See if you can find those feelings in your body.

2. Get together with a trusted friend and agree to give each other 10 minutes of attention. During your 10 minutes, talk about something you have strong feelings about. Allow yourself to feel your feelings as you share.

3. Practice noticing how you shut your feelings down throughout the day. What do you tell yourself or do to get the feelings to go away? Spend some time paying attention to how you allow or don't allow yourself to feel. Are there certain feelings you just won't allow? Take notes for a few days on this practice and process.

DISCUSSION for Episode 10
Reflections and questions to ponder alone, with a trusted friend, mentor, or group

1. What was your reaction to Rythea and Samantha talking about feelings?

2. What is your relationship to your emotions?

3. Are you aware of stuffing your feelings down? If so, what do you notice about it?

4. Are you scared of your feelings? If so, which ones scare you the most?

5. What did you learn about feelings when you were growing up?

6. What was it like to see Rythea and Samantha doing Peer Counseling and expressing big feelings with each other? Did it make you feel things? Did you feel resistant to it? If so, why?

7. Do you feel you have access to anger, sadness, shame, happiness, or fear? Which feelings are easiest for you?

8. Could you imagine doing a Peer Counseling structure with a friend? If yes, say more. If no, why not?

9. What was it like seeing the young kids on the video expressing some feelings?

Behind the Scenes of Episode 10

When I conceived of my online show, I dreamed of co-hosting with my friends because that sounded like the best thing ever. Making Episode 10 with my best buddy Samantha Burnell was as fun as I had imagined. It wasn't just easy fun, it was the kind of joy that comes from sharing what you truly believe in, concepts that changed our lives and we believed could change other people's lives as well.

We got separated and divorced from our husbands around the same time and became indispensable to each other during that period. We began practicing what we now call Peer Counseling (based on Re-evaluation Counseling). It's a listening structure that also focuses on the release of emotions. We met regularly to do this and did sessions on the phone. This practice rescued us during a time of great pain and turmoil. We both discovered that if we could keep feeling out loud and sharing about what was happening, we could get through one more day. It was an absolute blessing to have the skills of emotional release as well as the deep support of each other's closeness and attention.

On Episode 10, we discuss the purpose and advantages of expressing feelings. We talk about how stuck our life-force gets when used to hold our feelings down. We talk about how when feelings start to move, even painful, horrible feelings, life-force is freed up for living, for expressing, and for being present. Then we show this process on film, which at the time, felt radical. I felt like we opened a secret room and allowed viewers to see what it is like- the intimacy and the unkempt mess of it.

I felt so vulnerable when we made this, but I also knew it was a powerful modeling of what is usually forbidden. Free expression, especially anger, is often not allowed, not ok. Here we were, letting it out. Even a few seconds of it on film seemed like a wild dare.

Then our kids did the same thing on film, showed how it looks to freely express emotions. We had a wonderful, rich time doing this with our children, a creative project with meaning. The message we hammered at was, you must feel to heal, and this is how it looks.

Next Step: Now that you tapped into your feelings and noticed the ways you don't allow your feelings, you are ready for the next teaching, bringing self-love to the places that hurt.

Episode 11 of Advice from a Loving Bitch
Love is Universal

The Essence of Episode 11: Episode 11 brings back special guests from Episode 3 who so courageously aired their voices of self-hatred. They have returned with a totally different assignment, bringing loving confrontation to the places of self-hate.

The Teaching: In this episode, the special guests take time to demonstrate 2 things:

1. First, they talk back to their Self-Hating Voices by modeling the power and healing possibilities of contradicting painful, old, and debilitating messages. This is similar to the style of talking back that Rythea showed us in Episode 5.

2. Second, they talk directly to their Inner Child, telling the kid they once were, how precious and lovable they have always been.

There are certain ways of processing that facilitate repair work within us. They assist us to bond and re-parent ourselves.

Guests Flávia, Tom, and Rose show us the whole process so that you can see how individualized it can be.

These two exercises (on episode 11 and 12) are the tools to counteract the self-hating voice when we become the Loving Adult who says things such as, "No, this isn't true, I am not a failure, it wasn't my fault, I don't deserve to be left out, I am not ugly, I am not bad, I am not doomed, things are not hopeless for me, I am not destined to lose." This act of standing up is essential for stepping out of the heavy, crushing voices of meanness inside that are constantly telling us lies.

Healing is not passive, and it's not even possible until we engage with it full on. Once our parents or other trusted adults failed us in certain emotional ways, it is up to us to step in and finally be the Loving Adult we have been secretly waiting for. This episode shows you how to see the child you once were and say the things that child is still waiting to hear such as, "you are lovable and always were," "you are the best part of me," "you have helped so many people by being you," " you are so creative," and "you are such a bright being."

This practice is profound and transformational, but you have to really do it to get the benefit.

ASSIGNMENTS for Episode 11

The Assignment: The assignments for this episode ask you to retire your Self-Hating Voice in a loving way, and then reflect to your Inner Child who they truly are. All parts of this assignment go together.

1. Take a few moments to bring up the Self-Hating Voice and speak it out loud, then talk back to it like you heard the people do in this episode and tell it in your own way it's being retired. Be loving but firm. It's fine to do this exercise in writing if you find it too hard to say it out loud.

2. Find a photo of yourself as a little kid that you think is adorable and innocent. Look at the photo and tell that kid who he, she, or they really are inside, what you appreciate about the essence of that child. Be as loving as possible. It's fine to do this exercise in writing if you find it too hard to say it out loud.

3. If you feel very stuck bringing love and limits to your Self-Hating Voice, you can find a buddy to do this exercise with. I suggest watching Episode 11 together and then attempt to step in as the loving adult for each other either through

writing or speaking out loud. You can talk back to their Self-Hating Voice and they can talk back to yours.

4. If you feel very stuck looking at the photo of your little child and saying loving things to them, you can get a friend and ask them to do it for you and then see if you can internalize that loving behavior. They can look at the photo of little you and tell that child how lovable and good they are. Then you can try it yourself. Being loving and seeing the Inner Child's preciousness takes practice because you've been beating that child up for a long, long time. Be patient and keep at it.

DISCUSSION for Episode 11

Reflections and questions to ponder alone, with a trusted friend, mentor, or group.

1. What was it like to see the guests talking back to their self-hating voices?

2. What guests did you relate to and why?

3. Could you imagine talking back to your Self-Hating Voice? If so, what would you say?

4. Did you find the exercise humorous or liberating to watch? Say more about this.

5. What did you feel when you saw the guests saying loving things to their Inner Child? Did it stir up anything for you?

6. What are some of the things the guests said to their Inner Child that touched you or inspired you?

7. What might you say to the child inside of you?

8. Did you do the assignments? If so, what worked well for you and what was difficult?

9. How do you think your culture (school, media, peers, family, etc.) influences your Self-Hating Voice?

10. How have you internalized another person's opinion of you as a child?

Behind the Scenes of Episode 11

I'm a therapist, so I teach the skills from Episode 11 and 12 to my clients regularly, but it was important to see if my friends (who are not my clients) could step into these tools and find them effective without any preparation. They are my friends so they did have some exposure to my perspective on healing and on the show itself, but none of us knew what it would feel like to spontaneously attempt these exercises on camera.

I was amazed at their ability to stand up to the Self-Hating Voice with such love and commitment. They didn't hold back, they didn't flounder; they seemed to know just what to do. You can see during these episodes that big feelings were evoked, and a healing energy came through the process. So, it was a successful experiment based on years and years of my own work and practice.

For me, no matter how long I've been on this path to loving myself, there's always a deeper cut of healing. I took out a photograph of me at 5 years old for this episode and had my own big feelings about that hurt and terrified child. I felt relieved to tell her again that she's safe now, that she's a good person, and that she's loved. As corny as that may seem, I never tire of it or fail to get the benefits. The relentless (often unconscious) practice of judging myself needs regular contradictions of love, care, recognition, and re-parenting.

Next Step: You are learning the nuts and bolts of practicing self-love, developing tools you can use every day. Go to Episode 12 to continue to strengthen those tools.

Episode 12 of Advice from a Loving Bitch
Love Demonstrated

The Essence of Episode 12: Episode 12 is part two of Episode 11 and brings back more original guests who once bravely modeled the Self-Hating Voice at the beginning of the series. Guests Kent and Carrie, who express themselves very differently and come from different walks of life, show us how unique each person's process can look.

The Teaching: In this episode, Kent and Carrie have their own flavor of speaking back to their Self-Hating Voices. They demonstrate the inner strength and compassion needed to assert the Loving Adult. We get to see photos of them as children and begin to witness the powerful sweetness, vulnerability, and courage that all children possess. This episode is a chance to cultivate transformation by bringing love to our wounded parts.

ASSIGNMENTS for Episode 12

The Assignment: If you did the assignment from Episode 11, I suggest you do it again in whichever medium you haven't tried. If you did it through writing, I would do the exercise saying it out loud (some people even like to video themselves talking back to the Self-Hating Voice). If you said it out loud, try writing it out. It helps if you act out or write out the Self-Hating Voice first before you respond to it. All parts of this assignment go together.

Example: Writing out talking back to the Self-Hating Voice

Self-Hating Voice: You're a terrible mother. You are messing up your kid's life. You make so many mistakes and it's inexcusable.

Loving Adult: I'm so sick of you telling me that all the time. It's draining me. I'm not going to let you do it anymore. It's not even true. I'm an excellent mother and I'm not perfect so just stop.

Self-Hating Voice: I think it's obvious that you don't love your daughter right, you don't love her unconditionally, and you don't help her feel good about herself.

Loving Adult: You are a perfectionist, and you remind me of my perfectionist parents and this culture that is so hard on parents. I'm not going to argue with you, I'm allowed to be imperfect and to get support and that's enough. I'm good enough and she's good enough, and you don't get to evaluate me this way anymore. I know you are scared but your meanness is not helping us.

This dialogue can be however long, long enough to practice and strengthen the Loving Adult voice.

Example: Writing out talking to the Inner Child

Dear little me at 5 years old,

I know that a wounded part of me is always telling you that you are not good enough. I know that I tell you that you are a failure and that you will never make up for how unlovable you are. I know I push you and constantly worry. The truth is, we did get through our childhood and you were instrumental in getting us free. You were always so strong and courageous. You fought for what was right and you never gave up! You fought for all the gifts and talents that now come so naturally to us. You are such a beautiful fighter. You ARE good enough. You don't have to be perfect. You are so lovable!! I see you. I see who you have always been. I'm sorry I don't see it a lot of the time. I'm sorry our parents never really saw who you were and that I do the same thing. I'm going to change this and spend more time seeing who you really are.

Write a note to your Inner Child for at least 10 minutes.

DISCUSSION for Episode 12
Reflections and questions to ponder alone, with a trusted friend, mentor, or group.

1. How do you think oppression affects the Self-Hating Voice? For example, racism, sexism, transphobia, ageism, homophobia, and/or ability access.

2. Is your Self-Hating Voice expressing institutionalized oppressions (such as the ones mentioned in question 1) towards you? If so, what is it saying?

3. Did you notice how the guests in episodes 11 and 12 were giving voice to internalized societal oppressions such as racism, sexism, and ageism? If yes, what did you notice?

4. How do you discern if your Self-Hating Voice is saying the truth or is lying to you? How can you tell the difference?

5. What feelings does the Self-Hating Voice make you feel?

6. When you are loving towards your Inner Child, what feelings does that bring up for you?

7. Which feels better, the Self-Hating Voice or the Loving Adult? Talk about this.

8. How do we battle and contradict systematic oppressions that we have internalized? Any ideas?

Behind the Scenes of Episode 12

More and more, I wonder about how our Self-Hating Voice is and was designed to keep us compliant. Our parents, teachers, peers, bosses, government, and institutionalized systems of oppression have needed our participation in order to function. We had to cut off parts of ourselves in order to get love and attention, and to survive. We learned to hate parts of ourselves so that we would act and be how our caregivers and environment needed us to be. If our teachers needed us to be quiet and accommodating, we had to cut off the parts of us that were loud, defiant, physically rebellious or free. We had to cut off the parts of us that didn't want to learn what we were being taught. We were conditioned to like and reward the parts of us that other people liked and rewarded. That's how it worked.

If our parents needed us to be good listeners, good eaters, polite, happy, strong, fearless, exceptional, shut-down, helpful, successful, numb, invisible, bright, and/or bold, then we had to figure out how to give that to them in order to survive. Our parents liking us meant our parents taking care of us and that was a vital fight for life. We developed our sense of self by growing a Self-Hating Voice that worked tirelessly to get rid of the unlikable aspects of our personalities. We learned to mold and change ourselves around what would keep the bond with our parents and then with our world. The Self-Hating Voice was a huge part of how we did that.

Often, our environment taught us how to hate on ourselves through the systematic oppression that we were living in. For example, I learned to hate and judge my body as a girl and then as a woman through systematic sexism. I also learned to hate myself through anti-Semitism, and internalized anti-Semitism as part of my Self-Hating Voice.

My point is that the Self-Hating Voice had a purpose. A self-protective, surviving purpose. We can't just get rid our self-hatred like an ugly birthmark we are ready to remove. We must understand it first and respect its original function. We must have compassion for why we needed to hate ourselves in the first place and how it saved our lives. We must grieve and rage about the parts of us we had to hide in order to be safe. We must care for the child inside who still longs to bring all those ugly, out-cast, unwanted parts into the light of day. Then, we must let those parts be expressed. Our needy, angry, wounded, whiny, jealous, demanding, lonely, helpless, sad, and fractured parts are still there. Though they were once banished, they are still alive inside of us. We can love even the most hated parts of our personalities, and when we do, there is great relief, release, and repair.

Next Step: This process gets deeper and deeper as we go. We begin to see how our personal process is connected to the larger societal patterns of pain and oppression. In Episode 13, you'll look into your story and how that factors into this process.

Episode 13 of Advice from a Loving Bitch
Rythea's Story

The Essence of Episode 13: Rythea Lee takes a departure from the expected structure of the episodes and presents a film-short that tells her story of healing childhood trauma through dance, art, and performance.

The Teaching: Rythea spends this episode modeling what healing can look like and sound like. She tells her story of healing from childhood sexual abuse, sharing her experience of how movement and expression saved her from debilitating trauma. This episode is a claiming of Rythea's maturity and full living, with the clear encouragement to her viewers that healing is possible for them as well.

ASSIGNMENTS for Episode 13

The Assignment: This assignment gives you the opportunity to tell your life story in some organic way. Even if you think you know your story, it is always changing. If you find this assignment compelling, you could do it many times and see what aspects of your life story want to be told. What matters now that didn't matter 10 years ago? What aspects of your story have the most charge for you? Try it out and see.

1. Begin a 10-minute timed writing with the prompt "This is my story of healing…" Start with that prompt and write for 10 minutes (set a timer) without stopping, editing, or concerning yourself with spelling. When you get stuck, write the prompt again and go from there. Write about the thread of healing that has been woven through your life or write about whatever arises from the prompt.

2. *(Optional)* Read or share your writing with someone who cares about you. This writing exercise is fun to do in pairs so that you can both share what you wrote. Share to discover something about yourself and each other, and not to evaluate the writing.

DISCUSSION for Episode 13

Reflections and questions to ponder alone, with a trusted friend, mentor, or group

1. What did you learn from Rythea's story? Did it spark any thoughts, feelings, insights, and/or fears?

2. If you were going to tell your story, how might you tell it? Through film, writing, painting, collage, music, poetry, etc.?

3. What would be the trajectory of your story of healing? Do you have a healing story about how you survived? What did you use in your life and world to heal?

4. What did you notice about the dancing Rythea did in the video both alone and with her friend? Was any of it new to you?

5. What do you think it means to "tell your own story?"

6. What was something Rythea said in her story that stuck with you?

7. What was uncomfortable, scary, or difficult about hearing or seeing Rythea's story?

Behind the Scenes of Episode 13

Making this episode was a profound experience. First, just outing myself as an incest survivor was major. I was scared and excited to be that honest. For me, everything I've achieved and mastered is miraculous in the face of what I've lived through. I wanted to share my own amazement that healing is possible after impossible events.

I took my computer out to a nearby warehouse with high ceilings, strange corners, hidden benches, and filmed myself dancing. I also filmed myself in front of my house and on the porch, dancing. It was a warm day and it felt like a magical artist date with myself.

For another section of the episode, my friend Sanford Lewis, who is a filmmaker whom I adore, agreed to film Anna Maynard and myself dancing in a studio doing Contact Improvisation. Contact Improvisation is a dance form I've been practicing for over 20 years that is about bodies moving together through sharing weight. It's a very fluid, fun, spontaneous, and intimate form that requires physical play. I love it so much and I wanted to show the healing power of moving that way with others. I felt very vulnerable the day we shot that part, because I knew that I would be sharing this footage in the context of a bigger story. Still, it was lovely to film that day, easy and playful.

I wrote a bunch of words to go with the footage that I recorded with my editor, Tom Knight. He is a master at putting the elements together and it came out like a little movie about my life. I was proud of it and when I released it to my viewers, I got more emails and texts about that episode than any I had made before. It really touched people and that brought me great satisfaction. Making art, being brave, showing my process, allowing myself to take risks, always serves to help me love myself more.

Next Step: Maybe you are starting to think about your story, a healing narrative about how resourceful you have been? This is a good time to go on to the next phase of learning about self-love.

Episode 14 of Advice from a Loving Bitch
Q and A Episode

The Essence of Episode 14: In this episode, Rythea reads questions from her viewers and answers them with humor, play, and passion as her friend paints her face and body.

The Teaching: In response to some very astute questions from her viewers, Rythea discusses boundaries, caretaking, activism, oppression, late-night blues, self-love, dealing with fear, and spirituality. Her main point is to allow yourself to have emotions and thus be available to set limits, take action, take a hard look at the world, and choose love over and over again. A few points she makes:

1. Rage is a useful emotion to explore in order to find a calm and relaxed way to say no.

2. Personal healing can lead to the recognition of oppressive internal and external patterns.

3. Self-responsibility and healing are a lifestyle, a daily practice, and something we make our lives about.

4. Fear is present when we heal, but it shouldn't stop us from expressing who we are and what we believe in.

ASSIGNMENTS for Episode 14

The Assignment: These assignments are about desire and risk-taking. This is to help you see how self-love is not just about our thoughts but about our actions. You can do all the assignments or pick 2 of them.

1. Write down 10 things you need to say "Fuck Y'all" to. Practice saying "Fuck Y'all" out loud to the 10 things on your list. Get your rage moving!

2. Write for 10 minutes (time it) about the connection between inner healing work and social justice work. You can start with the prompt "It starts with myself and then…." Look into the idea that self-responsibility can lead to acting on the behalf of others. How might that work in your life?

3. Write about what time of day is the best time for you in terms of self-love and why? Explore a schedule that might work for you for doing some inner healing work and implement it. Would it be 10 minutes a day in the morning? A half hour a day at lunch? Right before bed? What could you commit to in terms of spending time on your own self-

inquiry? If healing is a lifestyle, how does it factor into your daily schedule?

4. Write a list of 10 self-love practices you do or want to do. They can be big or small, like walk your dog, sleep in, work out, meditate, read books, be in nature, go back to school, go on dates, stop going on dates, make yummy food, etc. Notice the things you already do and the things you want to start doing or do more.

5. Write down 10 things you want to do but are too afraid to do. Pick one thing on the list and do that thing (this could be something small, like telling someone how you feel, or something big, like taking a trip to Alaska). Carrying out one of the things on your list may take time and need to be done in steps so the bulk of your assignment today is to commit to doing it and taking stock of what is required to carry it out. Tell someone you are doing this and ask them to be a witness, either from afar or up close. Evaluate the effects of having taken a risk despite being scared. You can write about it or discuss it with someone you trust.

DISCUSSION for Episode 14
Reflections and questions to ponder alone, with a trusted friend, mentor, or group

1. Which viewer question and answer stands out to you? Why?

2. Did anything surprise you or feel like new information in this episode?

3. How did the face and body painting effect your viewing?

4. What comes up for you when you think of saying out loud "Fuck Y'all?"

5. Do you think you need to practice being more of a bitch?

6. Was there anything Rythea shared that you disagreed with or wish had gone in another direction?

7. One of the questions posed to Rythea was "How is managing the Self-Hating Voice and loving our Inner Child related to contemporary activism and social justice work?" Please answer this question in your own way. How do you think these things are related?

8. Another viewer said they struggled to love themselves in the evening after a long day of practicing self-love. Do you relate to this problem? If so, how?

Behind the Scenes of Episode 14

I think this episode is hilarious! The face and body painting that Rose Oceania was doing while I talked was so fresh, alive, and part of the conversation. It put a creative spin on the episode both visually and in terms of rhythm.

I was improvising all the answers I gave, and I am tickled by the things that came out of my mouth. I did not pre-plan these answers and they were very dynamic. I'm pleased by this. I love the part (in the first question) where I say "Fuck Y'all" and give a bunch of examples of how people ask us to take care of them at our own expense, and how important it is to say NO. In the first question, I tackle the idea that expressing rage in a safe way will slowly lead to a good, grounded "No."

The next question posed by a viewer was about how our personal healing relates to activism and social justice. She wanted to know how loving the Inner Child or facing the Self-Hating voice leads to social change. I think it's important to note that systematic oppression is not an individual problem; it is a societal problem that we all consciously or unconsciously participate in, fight against, and/or are victims of. The point I made in this episode was that if we become conscious of our hurts, we can recognize how we replay them in our lives on ourselves and on others. For example, if you were hit as a child and then you find yourself wanting to hit your own child, your healing work (of the kind I lay out in this series) would prevent the passing down of an oppressive pattern. The idea is, if we work on our self-hatred and heal our patterns of self-harm or harm to others, we free up our abilities to recognize external hatred and harm that is happening in the world. If we take responsibility for our own healing, it can lead naturally to taking action socially and politically as well.

Someone named John asked in this episode "Is it simply a choice to love the self, to practice at it, and make that my morning sit?" I answered a simple yes on the show, but there's more to say. If you imagine the amount of programming in your body and nervous system to hate on yourself, you can also imagine the effort and practice it might take to do something different. Being loving is a constant practice for me. I focus on it all day, every day. When I forget, the pain gets loud. Being loving is what I care most about. Not being loving in a self-absorbed way but being loving in order to love the people close to me, to love the world at large, to love my clients, my students, my daughter, my neighbors, everyone I know, every stranger I meet, etc. Practicing self-love is the template to loving others. It just works that way.

Another viewer talked about how hard it is to be loving to herself at night and I answer by discussing the practice of self-love, how it's a muscle we need to exercise and strengthen. I say, "It's a lifestyle." What I mean by this is that it never ends, it will always be required, and we get better and better at it.

The last question on this episode is about how vulnerable I have been in my episodes, how raw and uncensored. This viewer wondered if I have been concerned about what people would think. She asked if I've been scared, and if so, how have I managed it? Has it been scary? OMG, YES! Making an online show where I say what I really think? Terrifying. Dancing, singing, making huge proclamations and publishing every bit of it? Fearful? SO MUCH! But, so what? I know about scared. But I also know that in order to be fully alive, we must recognize we are scared and do things anyway.

So, how have I coped with my fear?

In answer to this question, I talk about all my personal growth practices; therapy, peer counseling, dancing, singing, writing, tapping (a technique called Emotional Freedom

Technique), support groups, and how going after a lifestyle of healing has allowed me to open up to love. Receiving love, giving love - that is why I am here. Because my childhood was so brutally traumatic, I have had to utilize every tool, modality, and practice I could get my hands on, to build a life for myself. It has been a long, long road and worth every bit of input I found. I can say with confidence that continually choosing to turn towards my pain, to open in the face of pain, has been my greatest choice. Inside that pain was my joy. Inside my joy was the real me. I've now given the real me a voice, legs to dance with, words to speak with, people to care for, and a world to be part of.

Next Step: You are starting to have a working vocabulary around self-hatred and self-love. Now it's time to move forward to Episode 15 where the range of who you are is given some acceptance.

Episode 15 of Advice from a Loving Bitch
A-holes are Everywhere

The Essence of Episode 15: This episode is a very tongue-in-cheek monologue about being wounded. Rythea is in her car and talks about being unkind and selfish, and how relative her "asshole" behavior is.

The Teaching: The essence of this episode is that no one is perfect. Everyone has wounds. Everyone acts from their pain if they are human, every single one of us. How can we recognize our imperfections and attend to them with love and humor? If we know we will make mistakes and be assholes, what then? Is there a way to love ourselves while we fall, get up, and fall again? Also, we are bright, unique, powerful, and magic makers. As Rythea says in this show we are each "one of a kind." How do we see all of it, and love all of who we are, the good and the ugly?

ASSIGNMENT for Episode 15

The Assignment: This assignment asks you to ponder the difficult and the wonderful. We all struggle with the balance of these two aspects of life. Here's a chance to let both parts of life have some airtime and expression. All parts of this assignment go together.

1. Take 5 minutes (time it) and write about the pain in the world.

2. Take 5 minutes and write about the beauty in the world.

3. Take 5 minutes and write about the pain in you.

4. Take 5 minutes and write about the beauty in you.

5. Do an 8-minute free write, starting with the prompt "I'm all of it." Write about the range of who you are, the mix of pain and beauty. Focus on your humanity.

DISCUSSION for Episode 15
Reflections and questions to ponder alone, with a trusted friend, mentor, or group

1. What struck you as truthful during Rythea's car ride monologue?

2. What seemed provocative or challenging about her discussion on asshole behavior?

3. Did you see a way you might be able to laugh at your own wounded behavior? If so, can you give an example?

4. Could you imagine having compassion for your and other people's wounded actions and ways of being? If yes, what comes to mind?

5. Rythea talked about how you are a magic maker, a "one of a kind" essence of a person. Did you resonate with that? If so, how? If not, why not?

6. What is magical about you?

7. What is magical about the people in your life or around you?

8. What did the assignments bring up for you?

9. What about forgiveness and self-hatred? How do they relate?

10. Could you imagine forgiving yourself for your asshole ways?

11. What is one thing you could forgive?

Behind the Scenes of Episode 15

This episode was based on a live show I performed a year before making this episode. It was a very different experience doing it live and getting the instant feedback of laughter from the audience of 300 people. In this episode, I was in a car and it was more like acting; it was an interesting challenge. I had to really commit to the jokes without having any real feedback. I imagine this is how people must do it on sitcoms and such.

Something that comes up for me is how much I love to curse and how offensive that can be to people, especially since I'm a woman. It's particularly because it bothers people that I like to do it. I like the shock of cursing and how it puts people on edge because my underlying messages are uncomfortable. I talk about abuse, I talk about healing, I talk about hatred, and I talk about radical self-love. I'm not trying to be nice about these things. Many of these subjects feel deeply linked to survival and they are provocative. I am hoping to wake people up and if that means being a little obnoxious, good. It works for me, and it is part of how I express myself.

In this episode, I'm aware that I say the world asshole like…a bunch. It's either going to be funny to the viewer or rather abrasive, or both.

My main point is that we are all assholes in some way and that is a fact. We are all wounded and trying very hard not to be. Or maybe some of us gave up on that long ago. Maybe some of us have given in to a life of asshole-ness.

We are also, all of us, beautiful. We are bright, lovable and shiny. We have amazing qualities. We have the potential to change the world by loving the people in our lives every day, every minute. Some of us are working that muscle, the love muscle, as hard as we can. Some of us can't find the open heart. Some of us, have never been loved enough to be able to give it. Most of us are somewhere in between, floundering around like the vulnerable, flawed creatures we are. Most of us are gorgeous, worthy assholes, on the rich road of learning. On the rich road of becoming more of who we are.

Next Step: You are possibly beginning to make space for all your human qualities. Now it's time to get creative in Episode 16.

Episode 16 of Advice from a Loving Bitch
Creativity Explained

The Essence of Episode 16: This episode is a lively discussion of creativity and self-expression, and how they relate to our core needs. It tracks childhood creativity, the individual mark of each person, and the vital role creativity plays in healing self-hatred and cultivating self-love.

The Teaching: Creativity is a core need, an outgrowth of who we naturally are. Humans are creative. If they believe they have no unique impulses to make, it is because they have gotten hurt in various ways and been taught to suppress those impulses. They have been made to think that only some people express freely and call themselves artists. Rythea shows her daughter dancing, painting, and singing in this episode, demonstrating the lack of separation between development as a person and creative spark. Rythea explains the meditative, altered state of creative process, and it's potential to create joy and presence in life. Rythea says "It's your human right to express yourself and it is loving." That is Rythea's main point. Making art is an act of love.

Artist Dana Wilde joins the discussion in the later part of the episode and adds her viewpoint about how the Inner Child and creativity are linked. In early years, children can draw with their whole bodies, and make sounds without self-consciousness. As people grow up, they get wounded artistically through capitalism and societal values, which for the most part do not include the support of artmaking for all. Both Rythea and Dana assert that art does not have to be about product or performance, but about process and healing.

ASSIGNMENT for Episode 16

The Assignment: This assignment asks you to push into your creative side and give up trying to be any good at it. All parts of this assignment go together.

1. Whether or not you consider yourself an artist, take 10 minutes (time it) and make a horrible piece of art. A bad song, a bad piece of writing, a bad poem, etc. Go for cliché, ugly, and boring. Allow for awkward, unoriginal, and uncoordinated.

2. Pick another medium and do the same thing.

3. Optional: Try this with a friend. Collaborate in making a very bad piece of art together. Try 2 different mediums.

4. Evaluate the process through writing or discussion. Was it fun or scary? Did you make something you ended up liking? Did it matter? Did you remember anything about making art as a child? Would you do it again?

DISCUSSION for Episode 16
Reflections and questions to ponder alone, with a trusted friend, mentor, or group

1. How was it to hear about creativity as a core need and as something everyone is born capable of doing?

2. What feelings came up for you in this episode?

3. How did it feel to watch Rythea's daughter express freely? Did you feel inspired or did it bring up feelings of being blocked?

4. What creative outlet do you most relate to?

5. What creative expression feels natural to you?

6. If no creative outlet is compelling for you, can you discuss why that might be? Was there ever a time when you did feel creatively open or driven?

7. How did you get hurt or suppressed creatively in your life?

8. Did you do the assignment of making bad art? If so, what happened? Discuss this process.

9. What do you think about art as an outlet for healing?

10. How do you think creativity relates to self-love?

Behind the Scenes of Episode 16

This episode is near and dear to my heart and who I am. Creativity and creative process saved my life over and over, and so aiming to convince others of its value felt imperative! I felt so passionate when I was filming this and then to have my daughter be part of it brought it to another level of realness. You can see in the episode how much she and I connect through art. We dance all the time, we paint, we sing, we rap, and we write stories. For me, art is really the STUFF of life, the content and the guts of being alive. I think this episode conveyed that, especially in hitting the points about creativity as a process verse creativity as a product.

I truly don't understand how people can stand to exist without an outlet of some sort where you see your own voice as distinct from others. It's mind-blowing to think that each person on earth has their own special way of seeing and experiencing life, but it's true. Even when we create in a community, we bring our voices together to make something that has never been made. That is the power of making something from nothing; it creates newness again and again.

When I first started dealing with my childhood trauma, things felt very bleak to me. I was suffering from PTSD and the loss of many people in my life. I felt alone and scared much of the time. I had a best friend I danced with 2 or 3 times a week, and in those rehearsals, something very vital kept emerging. I came to see that death and life were happening instantaneously. As I was falling apart and losing big chunks of my identity, I was also birthing deep knowing inside of me. I believe it was that creative outlet that kept me from total despair, and eventually delivered my life's purpose to me. The purpose to heal, and to help others heal through art, therapy, and humor.

Next Step: Creativity is a birthright for everyone, even if it's a rocky road. Now that you have put your toe in the water of individual healing, it's time to look at some social justice issues and how they relate to the big picture of our healing process in Episode 17.

Episode 17 of Advice from a Loving Bitch
Racial Justice Episode

The Essence of Episode 17: In this post-election episode, Rythea explores the subject of waking up to racism as a white person. She talks to her friend Kent Alexander about his views and experience dealing with racism and being on a healing path.

The Teaching: Kent Alexander discusses what it's like to be a black man living in a "progressive, liberal" town, being awake to his lack of safety, and doing his inner healing work every day. Kent shares how he sits with his feelings of being victimized by systematic racism and yet not becoming a victim inside himself. He discusses the "circles of oppression" and how different oppressions intersect.

Rythea asks questions about showing up for racial injustice as a white person and facing her own internalized racism. Together, Rythea and Kent lean into the idea of self-love and becoming whole, wrestling with self-hate, while staying sober to racial inequality.

ASSIGNMENT for Episode 17

The Assignment: This episode was designed for white people primarily, with the assertion that the healing process requires understanding of the larger forces of oppression, specifically racism. These 4 questions below were written by Sarah Watts for white people, see other assignment below if you are a person of color. All parts of this assignment go together.

When discussing race, ask yourself these 4 questions:

1. Am I trying to change the subject?

2. Am I using inappropriate humor to deflect?

3. Am I getting defensive or angry?

4. Am I going out of my way not to focus on "the negative"?

5. (*Rythea is adding this one*) Let your Self-hating Voice write about the subject of racism. Keep in mind, it's only for you, not for anyone else, so don't censor yourself. See what you learn about having internalized racism. Use this to come out

of hiding about internalized racism so that you can speak back to it and bring in the truth.

6. Please extrapolate on the above 5 questions, allowing yourself to use them as a jumping off point for writing about internalized racism.

If you are a person of color, an assignment suggestion:

If you found this episode useful, supportive, challenging or unhelpful, all your responses are important.

1. Make a scribble drawing about this episode, be totally non-linear, and let your body move the pen. Scribble for 1 full minute.

2. Do a free write with the prompt, "My accomplice is someone who…"

3. Lastly, do an 8-minute free write about what you felt during and after this episode. Share it with a friend you trust.

DISCUSSION for Episode 17
Reflections and questions to ponder alone, with a trusted friend, mentor, or group

1. Discuss what feelings came up for you watching this episode and why.

2. Discuss the homework assignment and what you learned about yourself from each question.

3. Talk about who you related to in the episode, Kent or Rythea, and why.

4. Did you learn anything about systematic racism or internalized racism from this episode?

5. Did you have a strong positive or negative reaction to the subject of this episode and why?

6. If you are a white person, what are you willing to do in order to become an accomplice to people of color? Are you open to doing the reading that Kent suggested *(in the YouTube description)* or looking into your internalized racism through your Self-Hating Voice?

7. If you are a person of color, did you feel supported by this episode and if so, how? If not, why not?

8. What moments stayed with you from this episode?

Behind the Scenes of Episode 17

I'm certain this was one of the most challenging episodes for me. I pushed myself to talk about racism with Kent Alexander and I felt totally vulnerable doing it. I was very scared to do it wrong, to appear ignorant and idiotic, and to embarrass myself terribly. I came to see that most white people feel this way when they begin the process of taking racism apart and getting sober about their own apathy, complicity, and white privilege.

It was clear that I just needed to be imperfect and model for other people what it looks like to learn. Kent was clearly sharing, teaching, and enlightening me to his experience, and he did it with an open heart. I was listening, taking in, and humbling myself on film. It was scary, BUT it was very, very important to me and I'm super glad I did it.

I filmed this episode at the beginning of my journey of learning about racism, but I've been at it consistently since then. Watching it now, I see I've come a long way. I've learned so much about my white privilege and what systematic racism really is. I've learned to befriend people of color in a whole other way and to "call in" my white friends who are not facing this issue and ask them to show up with me. I've done some reading but have learned mostly through talking to friends, reading on the internet, in workshops, from podcasts (I love the podcast called "Seeing White" with John Biewen), educational videos, talking to people who are passionately engaged in activism, seeing theatre, and doing my inner work facing my prejudice and programming around racial equality.

This subject is one of the most painful I've ever tried to tackle. It hurts every day. The reality of racism in our government, in our schools, in the media, and in our criminal system, all of it, is so deeply heartbreaking. I feel helpless, frightened, and enraged about it. I also know that feeling white guilt is a stage in the process of learning but not the destination. I'm not saying I don't have any, but I work to go deeper than that. I ask myself regularly what am I willing to give up in order to fight for racism: my time, my thinking, my money, my comfort, my approval, and/or my safety?

This is an ongoing question that I answer in different ways all the time and through different actions. One thing I know for sure is that we cannot go on the way we have. White Supremacy and Patriarchy are breaking down and it's in service to justice. I'm working as fast as I can to be part of the solution and not part of the problem.

Next Step: Facing racial inequality is hard! We can't do it alone. Healing does not happen in isolation. Go to Episode 18 to learn more about togetherness along the healing path.

Episode 18 of Advice from a Loving Bitch
Asking for Help/Prayer Song

The Essence of Episode 18: We cannot heal in isolation. We are meant to connect as humans, to share our pain, our joy, our fears, and our victories. Rythea discusses her history with being in crisis, getting help, and using "prayer" as another way to ask for support.

The Teaching: We learn as a culture that being in pain, or being less than functional, is shameful. We learn to hide out when we are hurting and hating ourselves. This is exactly the opposite of what heals us long term. We can lick our wounds, protect ourselves, do deep introspection, retreat, process alone, and that can have transformative effects, but ultimately, humans need intimacy. They need connection and reflection. They need corrective experiences of closeness to learn what safety and love can feel like.

Rythea discusses spiritual connection; what it is, why it's valuable, and how it looks different for each person. Finding and using a spiritual resource is how we develop our own Loving Adult who becomes the caring voice inside of us.

ASSIGNMENTS for Episode 18

The Assignment: This assignment asks you to explore how you isolate and hide and then how you connect with others and get support. All parts of this assignment go together.

1. Write for 10 minutes about how you isolate or hide, prompt "I'm hiding because..." Don't worry about spelling, grammar, or being interesting. Just write from your heart and gut.

2. Write for 10 minutes about what you are connected to "I feel connected to…" Don't worry about spelling, grammar, or being interesting. Just write from your heart and gut.

3. Reach out for support or connection, to a family member, a community member, a friend, a counselor, or an organization who helps people. Support can be sharing how you feel, what you need, what is hard, or where you feel stuck. You don't have to be in crisis, and it doesn't have to be a long conversation. It's about the intention of reaching towards connection. Even ten minutes can make a difference towards feeling less alone.

DISCUSSION about Episode 18
Reflections and questions to ponder alone, with a trusted friend, mentor, or group

1. Do you isolate yourself when you are in pain? Share about this.

2. Are you good at reaching out for support and connection? If so, how do you do it and what is helpful about this?

3. What kind of support has changed your life?

4. When has isolating been destructive or scary for you? Give an example.

5. Is there a special person who has helped you heal? Talk about that person.

6. How do you think spiritual connection relates to healing from self-hatred?

7. How do you think spiritual connection relates to self-love?

8. What are your fears about connecting to a spiritual source?

9. What has gone well for you about finding a spiritual source?

10. Is there something like singing, making art, or something like prayer that is spiritual for you? If so, how does that manifest for you?

Behind the Scenes of Episode 18

Talking about my history is difficult because my trauma was so severe. I get concerned I'm going to lose my audience because people won't relate to my story or minimize their own issues when put up against mine. I mean, I don't talk to my family of origin and that's rare and very heavy. I wonder if people hear about that and just emotionally disconnect. I imagine it could feel confrontational to hear about someone choosing a "family of choice" over their nuclear family. I mean, who does that? But this is my story, and this is so much of who I am. I literally created an adult life from nothing. No family support, no money, and very little hope. I built something over 25 years that I am so proud of, including my own family with my own child. When I talk about spirituality, I'm not being airy fairy. This shit has saved my life.

Creativity is a constant prayer for me, including this show! I believe in exposing my vulnerability because that is what it takes to let love in. You have to be open; you have to be honest. It's risky and scary, but there is no other way to grow.

So, this episode is deep. It's about letting others see you when you feel most ugly and needy. It's about reaching for the light when you think you might drown.

I really love Kaitlin June's song that we share in this episode because it embodies prayer on a few different levels. We are a group using our voices. We are collectively asking for help from Spirit. We are engaged in a creative activity that helps us feel alive. We are sharing it with a larger community to say, "Healing is real, let's do it together!"

Next Step: Are you considering a new level of reaching for support? As we consider moving towards more connection with others, we go on to Episode 19 about radical healing in the face of trauma.

Episode 19 of Advice from a Loving Bitch
Three Women Rising

The Essence of Episode 19: This episode is about the very difficult subject of surviving childhood sexual abuse. Rythea Lee, and guests Aishah Shaidah Simmons and Donna Jenson, answer 5 questions about what the healing process looks like, its deepest challenges, and biggest rewards. **Trigger warning: This episode uses some explicit language to describe sexual assault and childhood sexual abuse.**

The Teaching: This episode talks about the heart-wrenching reality of surviving childhood sexual abuse at the hands of parents and other family members. The show is educational in that it gives information about healing, and the scope of recovering from violation and betrayal. It tackles the reality of being a survivor within a culture of denial, ignorance, and "blaming the victim" consciousness. This episode illustrates how friendship, solidarity, breaking silence, self-love, creativity, support, and humor are resources that turned these survivors into joyful activists attempting to end CSA in our world.

The 5 questions Rythea, Aishah, and Donna answer are:

1. What glimpse of your story is worth telling?

2. What is your activism on this subject at this point?

3. What do you find most challenging about the level of denial?

4. Can you say anything about joy?

5. How does self-hatred relate to childhood sexual abuse?

ASSIGNMENTS for Episode 19

The Assignment: This assignment invites you to observe your denial (we all have some denial) with curiosity and respect. There is also the chance to explore your thoughts and ideas about the power to heal. All parts of this assignment go together.

1. Do a 10-minute free write with the prompt "I need my denial because…." Open to learning about your denial without judgment while you do this writing. Don't worry about spelling, grammar, or being interesting. Just write from your heart and gut.

2. Do another 10-minute free write with the prompt "I know I have the power to heal because…"

3. If this subject was triggering (bringing up very challenging feelings and pain) for you, reach out to a friend or support person and talk about it with them.

4. Look at the reading list in the notes area of this episode and choose a book to read on this subject.

DISCUSSION for Episode 19

Reflections and questions to ponder alone, with a trusted friend, mentor, or group

1. How was it for you to watch an episode on this difficult subject?

2. What feelings came up for you?

3. Was there a story in this episode that you related to?

4. Did you learn anything new about childhood sexual abuse?

5. What is your awareness around CSA being a national and global epidemic?

6. Do you know what victim-blaming is? Can you talk about it?

7. Is there any part of CSA that you have experienced that you feel safe sharing? If so, please share.

8. What kind of resources do you imagine are needed to actively face abuse by a family member?

9. What inspired you about this episode? Anything?

10. The folks in this episode answered some specific questions. Did any of their answers surprise you?

Behind the Scenes of Episode 19

This was, not surprisingly, the hardest episode for me to make. My Self-Hating Voice went ballistic on me. I felt like I was going to be attacked in some violent way if I published this show. Every message of being silenced came at me like a meteor. My abusers' voices were loud and relentless.

The day of the filming of this, I was freaking out. I called one of my closest friends and asked him if I could get sued or legally harmed for publishing this. He reassured me that I was simply telling the truth. He said it's not illegal to tell the truth. He also asked me if I did get attacked in some way, would it be worth it? I decided it was worth it and I went into the woods to film. During the filming, I felt open, relaxed, and full of fire. This happens to me often when I am in right relationship with myself, my art, and my voice. I get expansive and it's as if my angels are talking through me. It's such an incredible experience of being an instrument for love.

I think I crashed hard after releasing this episode, but I don't remember that too well. I do remember that a relative of mine had only one comment which was "I wish you wouldn't curse so much; it really waters down your message." I remember thinking, "Well then, you are not my audience, my friend." And I meant it. If you don't like my cursing, you don't get it. My cursing is my voice! It's my passion. It's my body. It's me. So, fuck off.

Aishah Shahidah Simmons and Donna Jenson changed my life by being part of this episode. They blew me away with their courage. We were a total team and our conversations helped me know that what we were doing was profound and necessary. Solidarity is essential when healing from sexual abuse! We need each other in order to contradict the messages that we are crazy, we are lying, and that basically, no one cares. They showed me that we are powerful in a group, that our truth is beautiful, and that joy is possible. I love these women and survivors everywhere who have the bravery to speak up despite the collective shame of our world. It's not our fault that the adults in our lives failed us and hurt us. We are heroes and heroines and that cannot be denied.

Next Step: You made it through the most challenging episode of this series! You are a rock star. Now you can go to the last episode, Episode 20, and integrate all that has happened.

Episode 20 of Advice from a Loving Bitch
Season Finale

The Essence of Episode 20: This is the last episode of Season 1 of *Advice from a Loving Bitch*. It is a recap of all 20 episodes interspersed with video comments from viewers who were following the show.

The Teaching: The clips from each episode trace the arc of the show and its teachings. We revisit the subjects of:
- Finding the Self-Hating voice
- Attacking the Inner Child
- Dialogue with the Loving Adult
- Talking to the Inner Child
- Talking to the Self-Hating Voice
- Getting in touch with our Essence
- Embracing Emotions
- False Beliefs
- Rythea's story of healing through the body
- Facing Racism
- Creativity
- Getting Support
- Learning about Childhood Sexual Abuse

You also get to hear from viewers how they benefited from the episodes: what they learned, what stood out to them, and how they were inspired to heal.

ASSIGNMENTS for Episode 20

The Assignment: This assignment is an integration of this course and a chance to see what stayed with you. It's also a chance to commit to a practice of looking at your self-hatred and growing your Loving Adult on a regular basis. All parts of this assignment go together.

1. Do a timed writing with the prompt, "What I remember most is..." and integrate anything about the show that stands out to you. What sticks with you?

2. Watch any of the episodes you missed. They all fit together like a puzzle. Did you miss one?

3. Commit to a regular practice in relation to your self-hatred and self-love. Write it down. For example, what about a daily practice of writing out your self-hating voice for 10 minutes? Or a daily practice of talking lovingly to your Inner Child in the mirror? Or a weekly practice of checking in with a friend about your healing journey and how it's going? Commit to showing up in a specific way and DO IT!

DISCUSSION for Episode 20
Reflections and questions to ponder alone, with a trusted friend, mentor, or group

1. What stands out for you about *Advice from a Loving Bitch*?

2. What has changed for you through watching this series? Any new awareness or habits?

3. What was the most challenging part of this series for you? Where did you hit the most difficult feelings or resistance?

4. What is valuable about AFLB? How was it helpful?

5. What episode do you think of when you think of the show and why?

6. Who did you relate to as a guest on the show?

7. What part of your Self-Hating Voice was a surprise for you?

8. Were you able to grow a Loving Adult voice?

9. Could you feel your Inner Child?

10. What are your main blocks to being able to love yourself?

11. Can you see the benefit of doing the practices Rythea demonstrated? Which ones and why?

12. Were you able to laugh during this show? If so, what made you laugh?

Behind the Scenes of Episode 20

I've been a counselor for 25 years, and I can confidently say that healing is real and possible. People do change, grow, evolve, and emerge from profound life challenges. With the right tools, support, and loving input, people find the courage to face the most threatening emotional material. Self-hatred is the biggest edge for most of us.

The tools I use with my clients and myself are unconventional, to say the least. I've always wondered if there was a way to trick the masses into engaging in therapeutic process, and this show was my master plan towards that end.

As you may know, I'm also a performer, a comic, and an instigator. *Advice from a Loving Bitch* attempted to use these talents to give the average soul searcher some basic tools. I knew I had to be entertaining and funny to hook people in. I had to be competent enough to explain why people should try out my ideas even though they are very vulnerable and edgy.

As I say in the beginning of Episode 20, I lived each teaching I offered in this series. I went through the tools as if I had never done them before (and I had!) and I found it to be a wild, heart-wrenching experience. Facing self-hatred is fucking the hardest! Self-hatred leads to traumas we buried. It leads to wounds we hoped to deny forever. It highlights terrible parenting or lack of adult guidance. It's ass kicking.

The tools of self-love were powerful for me in this show. I stepped into my maternal, unconditional, yet fierce voice, not just for me, but for my viewers. I wanted to embody what love can look and sound like. I wanted to be that parental role that I never had, that so many of us didn't have. It felt amazing!!! It changed me forever.

Episode 20 kind of blew my mind when I saw it finished. It showed me what a HUGE journey I had embarked on with myself, my guests, my daughter, my computer, my body, and my creative process. I had jumped into a project with complete unknowns at every turn. I didn't even know how to edit film when I began! I'm so grateful to the hundreds of people who emailed me about the show while it was being made. I got so much incredible feedback which is why I wanted you to see some of them on this last episode. People were touched by the material in many ways. Since I made the show, several people have used the videos for curriculum in colleges, schools, and online programs. People are seeing the value of AFLB as part of larger teachings on health, therapy, creativity, transformation, and community support. Thank you to you who are reading this now, and those who return to the show repeatedly for help. You rock.

Next Step: Live your good life!

CPSIA information can be obtained
at www.ICGtesting.com
Printed in the USA
BVHW061926180122
626556BV00011B/374

9 781792 318672